Manuel McFeely

ADVANCED PYTHON COMMANDS

Become a programmer from scratch and learn the most important commands of the most popular programming language in the business world

TABLE OF CONTENTS

INTRODUCTION

Nowadays, there are many programming languages, so why should you use Python?

Well, Python is a powerful language.

It's free: You won't have to incur any expense to start programming in Python, just a little of your time and your PC.

It's portable: You can install it on your PC and have it wherever you go.

It's easy to use: Python is very simple, you can start learning it at any age. All it takes is a little bit of effort.

It's rich in libraries: Through PIP, Python lets you install lots of useful libraries. Graphical libraries to create 2D games (pygame), mathematical (NumPy, math, mathplotlib...), and many others. There are more than 200...

Graphic programming: Python allows you to build graphical windows that interface with the users of your programs. With the right libraries, it's easy to do just that;

Web development, AI, and more...

Today Python is used in many prominent IT market players.

NASA uses Python for control system development, Yahoo! has developed some internet services in Python, Google and Youtube use Python.

For all these reasons, it would be absurd to miss the opportunity to make such a programming language your own, wouldn't it?

In this book, you'll find all the most useful commands to use your Python at its best. These are already intermediate and advanced level commands, suitable for those already familiar with this programming language.

If, however, this is something new to you, I suggest you take a look at some quick online courses (there are many free ones) or the other volumes in this series, such as Basic Python commands or Get Starting Programming with Python. That way, you can get the most out of this manual.

That said, how about you start exploring?

Chapter 1.
INTERMEDIATE PYTHON COMMANDS

The intermediate Python Commands are as follows.

- **Conditional/decisions: They are used to choose between two or more values, such as if-else.**

Example:

if x=0:

Print "Hello, world."

Else:

Print "Hello, world in Else."

- **For Loop: When iteration and action have the same items, this Python command is used.**

Example:

```
for x in [ 1, 2, 3, 4, 5, 6]:

Print x;
```

- **While loop: If the condition evaluates to false for the first time, the while loop will never be executed.**

Example:

```
x =0

while x<10:

Print x,

X= x+2
```

- **Else in the loop:** Loop has optional else for execution.

Example:

```
for x in [ 1, 3, 5, 7, 9, 11]:

Print x

Else:

Print "In Else"
```

- **Break and continue statements: The break statement is used to exit the loop when a specific output is reached, while they continue statement continues with the following iteration.**

Example:

```
if x==0:

Print "X is 0"

Break

Else:

Print "X is greater than 0."
```

Chapter 2. ADVANCED PYTHON COMMANDS

The advanced Python Commands are as follows.

- **List techniques:** The different techniques available to in list to perform the function.

Example:

X [1, 2,3,4,5]

- >>> X.append (7)

>>> x

[1, 2, 3, 4, 5, 7]

- >>>X.insert (0, 0)

>>> x

[0, 1, 2, 3, 4, 5]

- >>> X.remove (2)

>>> x

[0, 1, 3, 4, 5]

- >>> X.pop (1)

```
>>> x
[2,3,4,5]
```

They are simple to use, write, and understand. It is quite adaptable and can assist in obtaining the desired outcome in a variety of ways. Python is a versatile and well-developed language that is one of the most widely used languages in automation today. The above instructions will provide you a quick overview of what python commands can do and how they can be used.

To achieve effective results, it must be well-managed and written. Python is a programming language with a sizable community behind it. It has a bright future in the IT business, both now and the future. Python commands are basic and straightforward for those who are familiar with object-oriented programming. Organizations also require higher levels of python to meet their goals, and workers with this expertise are making a lot of money.

Chapter 3. PYTHON VARIABLES AND DATA TYPES – A COMPLETE GUIDE FOR BEGINNERS

In this Python tutorial, we'll go through the different Python variables and data types.

We'll also learn how to convert one data type to another in Python and how to use local and global variables.

So, let's start with variables and data types in Python. Tutorial.

What are Python Variables, and How Do I Use Them?

A variable is a value's container. You can give it a name so you can refer to it later in the program.

The interpreter determines the data type based on the value assigned. A variable can always be changed to a different type.

If you save 7 in a variable, for example, you can afterward store 'Dinosaur.'

1. Naming Guidelines for Python Variables

There are certain guidelines for naming variables (called an identifier).

- A letter (A-Z/a-z) or an underscore (_) is the only way to start a Python variable.

>>> 9lives=9

Output
SyntaxError: invalid syntax

>>> flag=0

>>> flag

>>> _9lives='cat'

>>> _9lives

Output
'cat'

- The remaining characters in the identification can be letters (A-Z/a-z), underscores (_), or integers (0-9).

>>> year2='Sophomore'

>>> year2

Output

'Sophomore'

>>> _$$=7

Output

SyntaxError: invalid syntax

- Python and Python identifiers are case-sensitive. The terms "name" and "name" are not interchangeable.

>>> name='Ayushi'

>>> name

Output

'Ayushi'

>>> Name

Output

```
Traceback (most recent call last):
File "<pyshell#21>", line 1, in <module>
Name
NameError: name 'Name' is not defined
```

- Reserved words (keywords) cannot be used as identifier names.

and	def	False	import	not	True
as	del	finally	in	or	try
assert	elif	for	is	pass	while
break	else	from	lambda	print	with
class	except	global	None	raise	yield
continue	exec	if	nonlocal	return	

2. Assigning and Reassigning Python Variables

You do not need to declare the type of a Python variable to assign a value to it.

You give it a name that follows the guidelines in section 2a, then type the value following the equal sign(=).

>>> age=7

>>> print(age)

Output

7

>>> age='Dinosaur'

>>> print(age)

Output

Dinosaur

Age=Dinosaur, on the other hand, is illogical. Also, you can't utilize Python variables until you've given them a value.

>>> name

Output

```
Traceback (most recent call last):
File "<pyshell#8>", line 1, in <module>
name
NameError: name 'name' is not defined
```

However, the identifier cannot be placed on the right-hand side of the equal sign. The code below generates an error.

>>> 7=age

Output

```
SyntaxError: can't assign to literal
```

You can't attach Python variables to a keyword either.

```
1.    >>> False=choice
```

Output

```
SyntaxError: can't assign to keyword
```

3. Multiple Assignment

In a single line, you can assign values to many Python variables.

```
1.    >>> age,city=21,'Indore'
2.    >>> print(age,city)
```

Output

21 Indore

Alternatively, you can use the same Python variable to assign the same value to numerous variables.

```
1.    >>> age=fav=7
2.    >>> print(age,fav)
```

Output

```
7 7
```

This is how Python Variables are assigned values.

4. Swapping Variables

Swapping means interchanging values. To swap Python variables, you don't need to do much.

```
1.    >>> a,b='red','blue'
2.    >>> a,b=b,a
3.    >>> print(a,b)
```

Output

blue red

5. Deleting Variables

You can also delete Python variables using the
keyword 'del.'

```
1.    >>> a='red'
2.    >>> del a
3.    >>> a
```

Output

```
Traceback (most recent call last):
File "<pyshell#39>", line 1, in <module>
a
NameError: name 'a' is not defined
```

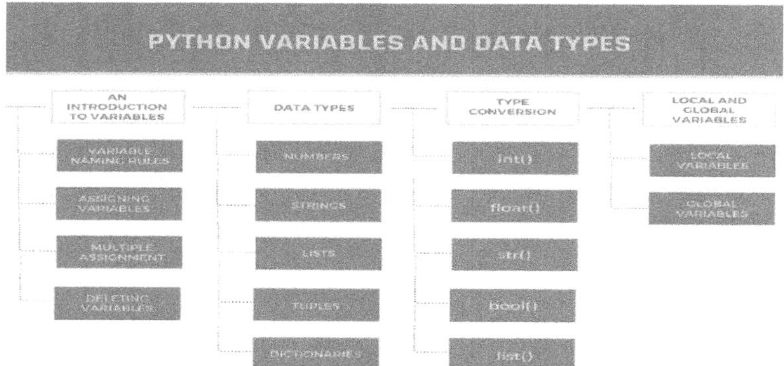

Chapter 4. PYTHON DATA TYPES

A value has a type, even if we don't have to declare one for Python variables. The interpreter needs this information.

Python supports the following data types.

1. Python Numbers

Python has four numeric data types.

a. integer is a kind of data.

Signed integers are stored in this Python Data Type. The type() function can be used to determine the class it belongs to.

```
1.    >>> a=-7
2.    >>> type(a)
```

Output

```
<class 'int'>
```

The sole constraint on the size of an integer is the amount of memory available.

```
1.   >>> a=999999999999999999999999999999
2.   >>> type(a)
```

Output

```
<class 'int'>
```

b. float

This Python Data Type stores real-valued floating-point values. The number 3 can only be stored in an int, although 3.25 can be stored in a float.

>>> a=3.0

>>> type(a)

Output
<class 'float'>

c. long

A long integer of any length can be stored in this Python Data type. However, in Python 3.x, this construct does not exist.

d. complex

A complicated number is stored in this Python Data type. The following is an example of a complex number: a+bj. The real and imaginary portions of the number are a and b, respectively.

>>> a=2+3j

>>> type(a)

Output
<class 'complex'>

To determine whether Python variables belong to a specific class, use the isinstance() function. The variable/value and the class are the two arguments.

>>> print(isinstance(a,complex))

Output
True

2. Strings

The term "string" means a series of characters. Python, unlike C++ or Java, lacks a char data type. To split a string, use single or double quotations.

>>> city='Ahmedabad'

>>> city

Output

'Ahmedabad'

```
1.    >>> city="Ahmedabad"
2.    >>> city
```

Output

'Ahmedabad'

a. Spanning a String Across Lines

You can use triple quotes to spread a string across multiple lines.

```
1.    >>> var="""If
2.    only"""
3.    >>> var
```

Output

'If\n\tonly'

>>> print(var)

Output

If
Only

>>> """If

only"""

Output

'If\n\tonly'

As you can see, the formatting was retained in the quotes (\n is the escape sequence for newline, \t is for tab).

b. Displaying Part of a String

A character from a string can be displayed by utilizing its index in the string. Remember that indexing begins with a zero.

```
1.   >>> lesson='disappointment'
2.   >>> lesson[0]
```

Output

`'d'`

The slicing operator [could also be used to show a string with a burst of characters.

```
1.      >>> lesson[5:10]
```

Output

'point'

This prints the characters from 5 to 9.

c. String Formatters

We can use string formatters to print both characters and values at the same time. The percent operator can be used.

```
1.      >>> x=10;
2.      >>> printer="Dell"
3.      >>> print("I just printed %s pages to the printer %s" % (x, printer))
```

Or you can use the formatting technique.

```
1.      >>> print("I just printed {0} pages to the printer {1}".format(x, printer))
2.      >>> print("I just printed {x} pages to the printer {printer}".format(x=7,
        printer="Dell"))
```

A third option is to use f-strings.

```
1.      >>> print(f"I just printed {x} pages to the printer {printer}")
```

d. String Concatenation

You can concatenate(join) strings.

```
1.    >>> a='10'
2.    >>> print(a+a)
```

Output

1010

You cannot, though, concatenate values of various types.

```
1.    >>> print('10'+10)
```

Output

```
Traceback (most recent call last):File "<pyshell#89>", line 1, in <module>:
print('10'+10)
TypeError: must be str, not int
```

3. Python Lists

A list is a collection of items with the same value. Keep in mind that it could include a variety of values.

Values separated by commas must be enclosed in square brackets to define a list. A list does not require the declaration of a type.

```
1.    >>> days=['Monday','Tuesday',3,4,5,6,7]
2.    >>> days
```

Output

['Monday', 'Tuesday', 3, 4, 5, 6, 7]

a. Slicing a List

The slicing operator may be used to slice a list in the same way that it can slice a string.

```
1.    >>> days[1:3]
```

['Tuesday', 3]

As a string, indexing for a list starts with 0. Arrays do not exist in Python.

b. Length of a List

A built-in function in Python calculates the length of a list.

```
1.    >>> len(days)
```

Output

7

c. Reassigning Elements of a List

A list can be changed. This means you'll be able to reassign elements at a later time.

>>> days[2]='Wednesday'

>>> days

Output

['Monday,' 'Tuesday,' 'Wednesday,' 4, 5, 6, 7]

d. Iterating on the List

The for loop can be used to iterate over the list. We may access each element of the list one by one by iterating, which is quite useful when we need to conduct operations on each element of the list.

```
1.    nums = [1,2,5,6,8]
2.    for n in nums:
3.        print(n)
```

Output

```
1
2
5
6
8
```

e. Multidimensional Lists

>>> a=[[1,2,3],[4,5,6]]

>>> a

Output

[[1, 2, 3], [4, 5, 6]]

4. Python Tuples

A tuple is like a list. You declare it using parentheses instead.

```
1.    >>> subjects=('Physics','Chemistry','Maths')
2.    >>> subjects
```

Output

```
('Physics', 'Chemistry', 'Maths')
```

a. Slicing and Accessing a Tuple

A tuple is accessed in the same manner as a list is used. It's the same with slicing it.

>>> subjects[1]

Output

'Chemistry'

>>> subjects[0:2]

Output

```
('Physics', 'Chemistry')
```

b. A tuple is Immutable

The tuple in Python is immutable. You can't change the size of elements of a declared object once it's been declared.

>>> subjects[2]='Biology'

Output

```
Traceback (most recent call last):
  File "<pyshell#107>", line 1, in <module>
    subjects[2]='Biology'
TypeError: 'tuple' object does not support item assignment
```

>>> subjects[3]='Computer Science'

Output

```
Traceback (most recent call last):
  File "<pyshell#108>", line 1, in <module>
    subjects[3]='Computer Science'
TypeError: 'tuple' object does not support item assignment
```

5. Dictionaries

A dictionary is a collection of key-value pairs. Declare it using curly brackets and commas to divide the pairs. A colon should be used to separate keys and values (:).

```
1.    >>> person={'city':'Ahmedabad', 'age':7}
2.    >>> person
```

Output

```
{'city': 'Ahmedabad', 'age': 7}
```

The type() function works with dictionaries too.

```
>>> type(person)
Output
<class 'dict'>
```

a. Accessing a Value

To access a value, you mention the key in square brackets.

```
1.    >>> person['city']
```

Output

```
'Ahmedabad'
```

b. Change Elements

You can change the value of a key.

```
1.    >>> person['age']=21
2.    >>> person['age']
```

Output

21

c. List of Keys

To obtain a list of keys in the dictionary, use the keys() function.

>>> person.keys()

Output

```
dict_keys(['city', 'age'])
```

6. bool

A Boolean value can be False or True.

```
1.    >>> a=2>1
2.    >>> type(a)
```

Output

```
<class 'bool'>
```

7. Sets

A list of values can be included in a set. Curly braces
are used to define it.

>>> a={1,2,3}

>>> a

Output

```
{1, 2, 3}
```

It only returns one instance of any value that is present
multiple times.

```
1.    >>> a={1,2,2,3}
2.    >>> a
```

Output

```
{1, 2, 3}
```

A set, on the other hand, is unordered and so does not
support indexing.

```
1.    >>> a[2]
```

Output

```
Traceback (most recent call last):
  File "<pyshell#127>", line 1, in <module>
    a[2]
TypeError: 'set' object does not support indexing
```

It's also changeable. You can edit or add to its elements. To do so, use the add() and remove() methods.

>>> a={1,2,3,4}

>>> a

Output

{1, 2, 3, 4}

>>> a.remove(4)

>>> a

Output

{1, 2, 3}

>>> a.add(4)

>>> a

Output

{1, 2, 3, 4}

Type Conversion

Because Python is dynamically typed, you might want to change the type of a value. Python has several functions that can be used to accomplish this.

1. int()

It converts the value into an int.

>>> int(3.7)

Output

3

It's worth noting how it shortened 0.7 instead of rounding it to 4. A Boolean can also be converted to an integer.

>>> int(**True**)

Output

1

>>> int(**False**)

A string, on the other hand, cannot be converted to an int. It generates an error.

>>> int("a")

Output

```
Traceback (most recent call last):
File "<pyshell#135>", line 1, in <module>;
int("a")
ValueError: invalid literal for int() with base 10: 'a'
```

You can, though, if the string contains only numbers.

>>> int("77")

Output

77

2. float()

It converts the value into a float.

```
>>> float(7)
Output
7.0
>>> float(7.7)
Output
7.7
>>> float(True)
Output
1.0
>>> float("11")
Output
11.0
```

You can also use 'e' to denote an exponential number.

```
>>> float("2.1e-2")
Output
0.021
>>> float(2.1e-2)
Output
0.021
```

However, this number works even without the float() function.

```
>>> 2.1e-2
Output
0.021
```

3. str()

It converts the value into a string.

```
>>> str(2.1)
Output
'2.1'
>>> str(7)
Output
'7'
>>> str(True)
Output
'True'
```

A list, a set, a tuple, or a dictionary can also be converted to a string.

```python
>>> str([1,2,3])
Output
'[1, 2, 3]'
```

4. bool()

It converts the value into a boolean.

```python
>>> bool(3)
Output
True
>>> bool(0)
Output
False
>>> bool(True)
Output
True
>>> bool(0.1)
Output
True
```

You can convert a list into a Boolean.

```
>>> bool([1,2])
Output
True
```

The function returns False for empty constructs.

```
>>> bool()
Output
False
>>> bool([])
Output
False
>>> bool({})
Output
False
```

None is a keyword in Python that represents an absence of value.

```
>>> bool(None)
Output
False
5. set()
```

It converts the value into a set.

```
>>> set([1,2,2,3])
Output
{1, 2, 3}
>>> set({1,2,2,3})
Output
{1, 2, 3}
6. list()
```

It converts the value into a list.

```
>>> del list
>>> list("123")
Output
['1', '2', '3']
>>> list({1,2,2,3})
Output
[1, 2, 3]
>>> list({"a":1,"b":2})
Output
['a', 'b']
```

However, the following raises an error.

```
>>> list({a:1,b:2})
```

Output

```
Traceback (most recent call last):
File "<pyshell#173>", line 1, in <module>;
list({a:1,b:2})
TypeError: unhashable type: 'set'
```

3. tuple()

It converts the value into a tuple.

>>> tuple({1,2,2,3})

Output

(1, 2, 3)

You can try your own combinations. Also try composite functions.

>>> tuple(list(set([1,2])))

Output

(1, 2)

Chapter 5. PYTHON LOCAL AND GLOBAL VARIABLES

Another way to categorize Python variables is by their scope.

1. Python Local Variables

A variable declared in a function, class, or another scope is only visible in that scope. You get an 'undefined' error if you call it outside of that scope.

```
>>> def func1():

uvw=2

print(uvw)

>>> func1()
```

Output
2
```
>>> uvw
```

Output

```
Traceback (most recent call last):
  File "<pyshell#76>", line 1, in <module>
  uvw
  NameError: name `uvw' is not defined[/php]
```

The variable uvw is local to the function func1 in this case ().

2. Global Variables

A variable declared outside of any context/scope is visible throughout the program.

>>> xyz=3

>>> **def** func2():

xyz=0

xyz+=1

print(xyz)

>>> func2()

Output
1

>>> xyz

Output
3

In a local scope, the 'global' keyword can be used to treat a variable as global.

>>> foo=1

>>> **def** func2():

global foo

foo=3

print(foo)

>>> func2()

Output
3

>>> foo

Output
3

Chapter 6. PYTHON OPERATOR – TYPES OF OPERATORS IN PYTHON

In this Python Operator lesson, we'll look at what an operator is and how to use it in the Python programming language.

We'll go over the syntax and examples for the following Python Operators: Arithmetic, Relational, Assignment, Logical, Membership, Identity, and Bitwise Operators.

Let's get started with the Python Operators Tutorial.

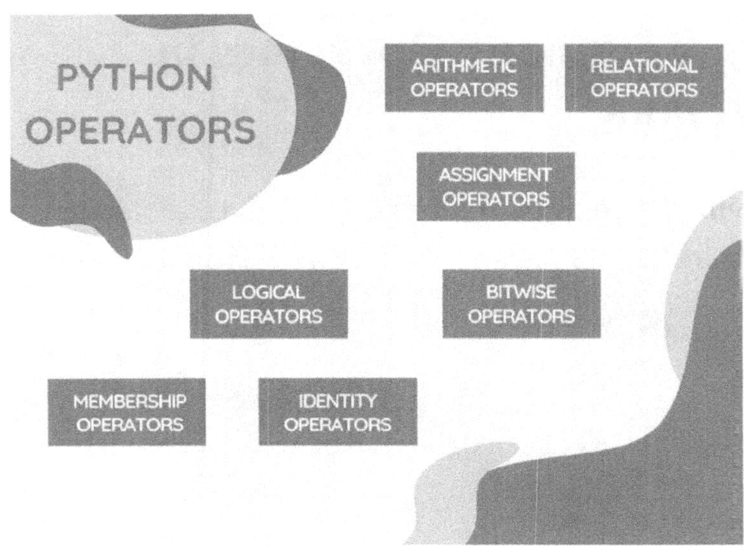

What does a Python operator mean?

An operator in Python is a symbol that performs a task on one or more operands. A variable or a value on which the operation is performed is referred to as an operand.

There are seven types of Python operators:

- Python Relational Operator
- Python Arithmetic Operator
- Python Assignment Operator
- Python Membership Operator
- Python Logical Operator
- Python Identity Operator
- Python Bitwise Operator

1. Arithmetic Operators in Python

Python operators for basic mathematical operations are included in this list of Python arithmetic operators.

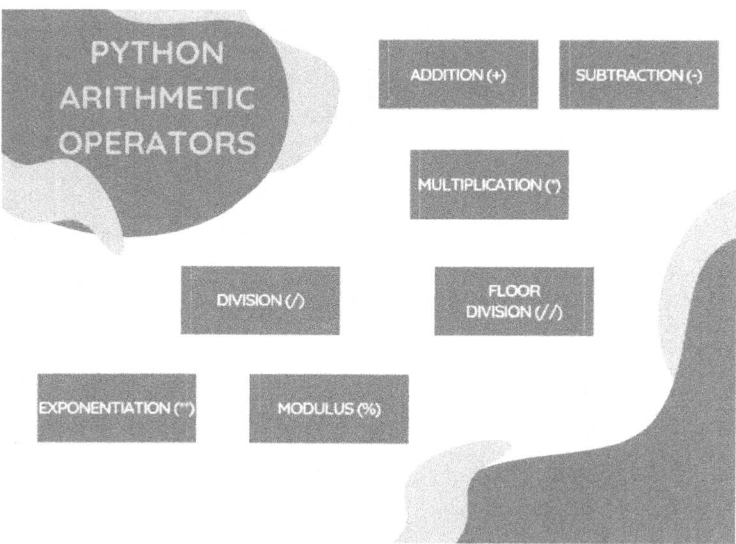

a. Addition(+)

The values on equal sides of the operator are added together.

```
>>> 3+4
Output
7
```

b. Subtraction(-)

Subtracts the right-hand value from the left-hand value.

```
>>> 3-4
Output
-1
```

c. Multiplication(*)

The values on equal sides of the operator are multiplied.

```
>>> 3*4
Output
12
```

d. Division(/)

Divides the left-hand value by the right-hand value. It's worth noting that division yields a floating-point value.

```
>>> 3/4
Output
0.75
```

e. Exponentiation(**)

Tends to raise the first number to the second's power.

```
>>> 3**4
Output
81
```

f. Floor Division(//)

Divides the quotient into integers and returns the result. After the decimal, it dumps the digits.

```
>>> 3//4
>>> 4//3
Output
1
>>> 10//3
Output
3
```

g. Modulus(%)

Divides the remaining and returns the result.

```
>>> 3%4
Output
3
>>> 4%3
Output
1
>>> 10%3
Output
1
>>> 10.5%3
Output
1.5
```

2. Python Relational Operator

The Relational Python Operator carries out the comparison between operands.

They indicate whether one operand is greater, lesser, equal, or a combination of the three.

a. Less than(<)

This operator determines whether the value on the left is less than the value on the right.

>>> 3<4

Output

True

b. Greater than(>)

It determines whether the value on the operator's left is greater than the value on the right.

>>> 3>4

Output

False

c. Less than or equal to(<=)

It determines if the value on the operator's left is less than or equal to the value on the right.

>>> 7<=7

Output

True

d. Greater than or equal to(>=)

It checks if the value on the operator's left is greater than or equal to the one on the right.

>>> 0>=0

Output

True

e. Equal to(= =)

This operator determines whether the value on the operator's left equals the value on the operator's right.

The Boolean value True is equivalent to 1 but not to 2. Furthermore, 0 equals False.

```
>>> 3==3.0
Output
True
>>> 1==True
Output
True
>>> 7==True
Output
False
>>> 0==False
Output
True
>>> 0.5==True
Output
False
```

f. Not equal to(!=)

It determines whether the value on the left of the operator differs from the value on the right.

The Python operator ◇ does the same function. However, it was deprecated in Python 3.

When the relative operator's condition is met, it returns True. Otherwise, False is returned. This return value can be used in another statement or expression.

```
>>> 1!=1.0
```

Output

```
False
```

```
>>> -1<>-1.0
```

#This causes a syntax error

3. Python Assignment Operator

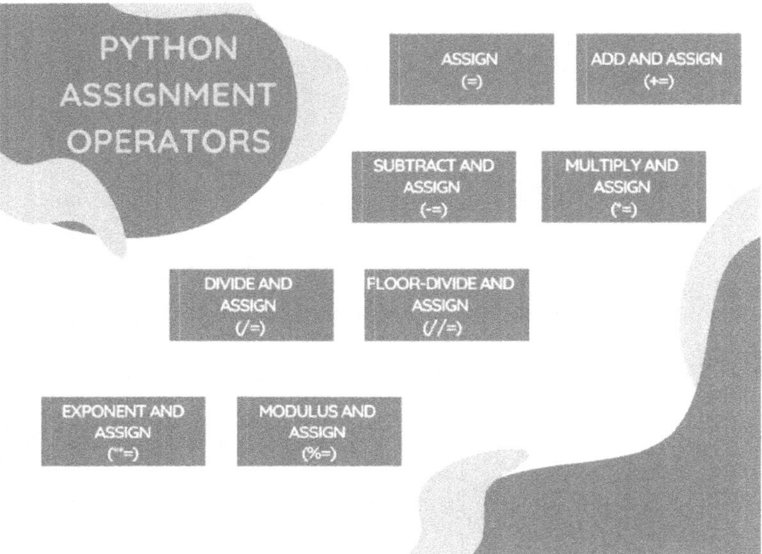

The Python assignment operator gives a variable a value. Before allocating the value, it may alter it by a factor.

There are eight assignment operators in total: one plain and seven for the seven arithmetic Python operators.

a. Assign(=)

Gives the expression on the left a value. It's worth noting that whereas == is used to compare, = is used to assign.

```
>>> a=7
>>> print(a)
Output
7
```

b. Add and Assign(+=)

Adds the values on both sides and assigns them to the left-hand expression. The expression a+=10 is the same as a=a+10.

The same may be said for all of the following assignment operators.

```
>>> a+=2
>>> print(a)
Output
9
```

c. Subtract and Assign(-=)

Subtracts the value on the right from the value on the left. Then it assigns it to the expression on the left.

```
>>> a-=2
```

```
>>> print(a)
```

Output

```
7
```

d. Divide and Assign(/=)

Divides the value on the left by the one on the right. Then it assigns it to the expression on the left.

```
>>> a/=7
```

```
>>> print(a)
```

Output

```
1.0
```

e. Multiply and Assign(*=)

Multiplies the values on either side. Then it assigns it to the expression on the left.

```
>>> a*=8
```

```
>>> print(a)
```

Output

```
8.0
```

f. Modulus and Assign(%=)

Performs modulus on both sides of the equation. The phrase on the left is then assigned to it.

```
>>> a%=3
>>> print(a)
Output
2.0
```

g. Exponent and Assign(**=)

Performs exponentiation on both sides of the equation. The phrase on the left is then assigned to it.

```
>>> a**=5
>>> print(a)
Output
32.0
```

h. Floor-Divide and Assign(//=)

Floor division is applied to the values on both sides. The phrase on the left is then assigned to it.

```
>>> a//=3
>>> print(a)
Output
10.0
```

This is one of the important Python operators.

4. Python Logical Operator

These are conjunctions that can be used to join two or more conditions together.

We have 3 Python logical operators: and, or, and not, all included in the Python operators category.

a. and Operator in Python

The expression as a whole is true if the conditions on both sides of the operator are true.

>>> a=7>7 and 2>-1

>>> print(a)

Output
```
False
```

b. or Operator in Python

Only if both of the statements surrounding the operator are false is the expression false. Otherwise, the statement is correct.

```
>>> a=7>7 or 2>-1
>>> print(a)
Output
True
```

'and' returns the first False value or the last value; 'or' returns the first True value or the last value

```
>>> 7 and 0 or 5
Output
5
```

c. not Operator in Python

This inverts an expression's Boolean value. True to False and False to True are both converted.

The Boolean value for 0 is False, as shown below. As a result, it does not invert to True.

```
>>> a=not(0)
>>> print(a)
Output
True
```

5. Membership Python Operator

These operators determine whether a value belongs to a sequence. A list, a tuple, or a string can be used to represent the sequence.

'in' and 'not in' are the two membership python operators.

a. Python's in operator

This determines whether a value belongs to a series.

We can see that the string 'fox' does not belong in the list of pets in our case. It does, however, belong to the string 'cat,' therefore it returns True.

In addition, the word 'me' is a substring of the word 'disappointment.' As a result, it returns true.

```
>>> pets=['dog','cat','ferret']
>>> 'fox' in pets
Output
False
>>> 'cat' in pets
Output
True
>>> 'me' in 'disappointment'
Output
True
```

b. not in Operator in Python

Unlike 'in', 'not in' checks if a value is not a sequence member.

```
>>> 'pot' not in 'disappointment'
Output
True
```

In doubt yet in any Python operator with examples? Please comment.

6. Identity Operator in Python

Let's move on to identifying the Python Operator.

These operators determine whether the two operands have the same identity. 'Is' and 'Is Not' are the two identity operators.

a. is Operator in Python

It returns True if two operands have the same identity. Otherwise, False is returned. Because 2 is not equal to 20, the result is False.

Also, the numbers "2" and "2" are the same. The differences in quotes do not distinguish them. As a result, True is returned.

```
>>> 2 is 20
Output
False
>>> '2' is "2"
Output
True
```

b. is not an Operator in Python

'2' is a string, and 2 is a number. As a result, it returns
True.

```
>>> 2 is not '2'
Output
True
```

7. Python Bitwise Operator

Let's have a look at the Bitwise Python Operator now.

These operate bit by bit on the operands.

a. Binary AND(&) Operator in Python

On the two values, it conducts a bit-by-bit AND operation. The binary value for 2 is 10, whereas the binary value for 3 is 11. When you & them together, you get 10, which is binary for two.

Likewise, &-ing 011(3) and 100(4) yields 000. (0).

```
>>> 2&3
Output
2
>>> 3&4
Output
0
```

b. Python's Binary OR(|) Operator

On the two values, it does a bit-by-bit OR. When you OR 10(2) with 11(3), you get 11. (3).

>>> 2| 3

Output

Output

c. Python Binary XOR() Operator

On the two values, it executes a bit-by-bit XOR(exclusive-OR). XORing 10(2) and 11(3) yields 01 in this case (1).

>>> 2^ 3 \sOutput

1

d. In Python, Binary One's Complement()

It returns the binary one's complement of a number. The bits are flipped. The binary code for two is 00000010. 11111101 is one's complement.

This is binary for -3. So, this results in -3. Similarly, ~1 results in -2.

>>>

~-3 \sOutput

2

The complement of -3 is 2, once again.

e Python's Binary Left-Shift() Operator

The value of the left operand is shifted to the left by the number of places specified by the right operand.

The binary of 2 is 10 in this case, which shifts it to two positions to the left. This yields 1000, which is the binary equivalent of the number 8.

```
>>> 2<<2 \sOutput
```

f. Python Binary Right-Shift(>>)

The value of the left operand is moved to the right by the number of places specified by the right operand.

Here, the binary of 3 is 11. 3>>

2 shifts it two positions to the right. This yields the number 00, which is binary for zero.

Similarly, 3>>1 shift it to the right one position. This yields the number 01, which is binary for one.

```
>>> 3>>2
>>> 3>>1
Output
1
```

This was all about the Python Operator Tutorial.

Questions about Python Operators in Python Interviews

1. In Python, what is the not operator?
2. What are the several types of relational operators in Python?
3. What does!= in Python mean?
4. Describe the different types of Bitwise Operators in Python.
5. Describe the Python floor-divide and assign operators.

Finally, we looked at seven different types of Python operators in this course.

To see how they function, we ran them in the Python Shell (IDLE). This operator can also be used in conditions and to combine them.

Go ahead and experiment with some different combinations.

Chapter 7. MODULES VS PACKAGES IN PYTHON

This book is a compilation of the most significant changes in Python modules and packages. Many programmers struggle to determine when and where a module or package should be utilized.

A clear set of distinctions will be shown in this article, making it easier for the coder to work more efficiently with both modules and packages.

What are Python Modules?

A pythonic statement that comprises numerous functions is known as a module. Modules operate as a pre-defined library in the code that both the coder and the user can access.

While the code is being executed, the python modules additionally save pre-defined functions from the library.

Example of Python Module:

import math

from math import pow

pow(2,8)

print(pow)

Output:

```
<built-in function pow>
>>>
```

What are Python Packages?

A package is a collection of tools that aid in the initialization of a program. For any source code, a python package serves as a user-variable interface. This makes a python package work for every functional code in the runtime at a specific moment.

Example of Python Package:

import math

print("math package")

Output:
```
math package
>>>
```

Python Modules and Packages: What's the Difference?

1. Every user-oriented code is contained in a package, which contains the file init .py. However, this does not apply to any user-specific codes in runtime modules.

2. A module is a file that contains Python code that runs in the background for user-specific programming. A package also alters user-interpreted code so that it can be readily executed during runtime.

A python "module" is made up of a unit namespace and the variables extracted locally. There are also some parsed functions, such as:

- Variables and constants
- Property definitions by class
- Any old or new value.
- Typically, a module corresponds to a single file.

- In the user interface library, a debugging tool.

A few often used tools assist the coder in creating a new platform employing modules for efficient code execution. During runtime, this also installs and distributes packages throughout the library.

The package's well-structured and standard layout makes it simple to use user-specific utilities. It also makes runtime executions easier.

What distinguishes a Python Package from a Python Module?

What distinguishes a Python package from a module is a frequently asked question. A python package is a library that defines the codes as a single unit for any given function. The modules, on the other hand, are a separate library with built-in functionality. Packages are preferable to modules because of their reusability.

Explicit Namespaces are a type of namespace that is defined explicitly.

In the code that is processed for the first time, this supplies the default namespace. In the identification of the code, these namespaces serve as a source code. A new developer, on the other hand, can use the library to import them. However, knowing the generic namespaces is always a good idea for proper code execution.

```
def thisistech():

a='Greetings!'

thisistech()
```

Output:

```
>>> thisistech
<function thisistech at 0x030BFCD0>
>>>
```

Convenience API

This is a mechanism for namingspaceing specific objects in the code. It takes the user right to the heart of the code, making it simple to spot problems. This also aids in parsing the codes so that they can be used as user interface codes during runtime.

```
import hello

hello.hey()

'Hey, there!'
```

Output:

```
Error
```

Chapter 8. PYTHON FUNCTION ARGUMENTS WITH TYPES, SYNTAX, AND EXAMPLES

In this Python Function Arguments tutorial, we'll look at Python's several types of function arguments, including Python Keyword Arguments, Python Default Arguments, and Python Arbitrary Arguments.

Let's get started using Python Function Arguments.

What is a Python function, exactly?

A Python function is a set of statements that execute in a specific order and are given a name. We can reuse code as a result of this.

The keyword 'def' is used to define a function. Let's have a look at an example.

```
>>> def sayhello():
        """
        This prints Hello
        """
        print("Hello")
```

Then we simply put the function's name in parentheses to invoke it. Take note of the docstring as well.

```
>>> sayhello()
```

Output

```
Hello
```

This one does not accept any counter-arguments. Let's have a look at one with python function arguments.

```
>>> def sum(a,b):
        return a+b
>>> sum(2,3)
```

Output

5

The interpreter complains if just one argument is passed.

```
1.    >>> sum(3)
2.    Traceback (most recent call last):
3.    File "<pyshell#44>", line 1, in <module>
4.    sum(3)
```

Output

```
TypeError: sum() missing 1 required positional argument: 'b'
```

Different types of parameters are used in python functions to deal with such circumstances.

Python Function Arguments Types

Python arguments functions come in a variety of shapes and sizes. Let's go over each one by one:

1. Python Program Arguments with Default Values

Python Program arguments can have default values. The assignment operator in Python(=) is used to assign a default value to an argument.

When a function is called without a value for an argument, the default value (as previously stated) is used.

```
1.    >>> def greeting(name='User'):
2.                print(f"Hello, {name}")
3.    >>> greeting('Ayushi')
```

Output

```
Hello, Ayushi
```

>>> greeting()

Output

```
Hello, User
```

When greeting() is used without an argument, the name is set to its default value, which is 'User.'

A default value can be set for any number of arguments. However, you must avoid using a non-default option following a default argument.

To put it another way, if you supply a default argument, any others that succeed must also have default values.

The reason is straightforward. Assume you have a two-parameter function.

There is no default value for the first argument, but there is for the second. You simply have to submit one parameter when you call it now (assuming it was authorized).

It is the initial argument, according to the interpretation. So, what happens to the second point? It is completely oblivious.

```
>>> def sum(a=1,b):
```

```
return a+b
```

Output

```
SyntaxError: non-default argument follows
default argument
```

This was all about Python 2's default arguments.

2. Keyword Arguments in Python

In Python, keyword arguments allow us to modify the order in which arguments are sent without causing any problems.

Let's look at a function that returns the quotient when two numbers are divided.

```
>>> def divide(a,b):

return a/b

>>> divide(3,2)
```

Output

```
1.5
```

This function can be called with any number of parameters as long as we indicate which value goes into which.

```
>>> divide(a=1,b=2)
```

Output

```
0.5
```

```
>>> divide(b=2,a=1)
```

Output

```
0.5
```

As you can see, they both deliver the same result. These are keyword arguments for python functions.

However, placing a positional argument after a keyword argument will result in a SyntaxError Python error.

```
>>> divide(b=2,1)
```

Output

```
SyntaxError: positional argument follows keyword
argument in python.
```

Python Function Arguments: Any Doubts?

3. Python Arbitrary Arguments

You never know how many debates you'll face—an asterisk (*) is used before an argument name in this scenario.

```
1.    >>> def sayhello(*names):
2.                for name in names:
3.                        print(f"Hello, {name}")
```

The parameters are wrapped into a Python tuple when you call the function with several arguments.

The for loop in Python is used to cycle over them.

>>> say hello('Ayushi','Leo','Megha')

Output

```
Hello, Ayushi
Hello, Leo
Hello, Megha
```

The Python Function Arguments were the focus of this chapter.

Function Arguments Interview Questions in Python

1. What are Python function arguments?
2. In Python, how do you make a function argument?
3. In Python, how do you determine if a function is an argument?

4. What is a Python argument? Give a specific example.

5. What are the different forms of Python function arguments?

As a result, we may conclude that Python Function Arguments and its three sorts of function arguments. There are three types of arguments: default, keyword, and arbitrary.

Keyword arguments allow us to employ any order, whereas default arguments assist us to deal with the absence of values.

Finally, arbitrary arguments come in handy with Python when we don't know how many arguments we'll get.

Chapter 9. PYTHON REGULAR EXPRESSION FUNCTIONS

Regular Expressions in Python is one of my favorite topics. Let's get started with Python Regex Tutorial without wasting any time.

Metacharacters, samples, and functionalities of Python Regex will be discussed here. We'll also go over Python find all and Python multiline.

Let's get started with a quick Python Regex Cheat Sheet.

What is a regular expression (Regex) in Python?

A Python regular expression is essentially a string of characters that defines a search pattern.

Using this pattern in a string-searching technique, we can then "find" or "find and replace" strings. This feature is also available in Microsoft Word.

We will study the fundamentals of regular expressions in Python in this Python Regex lesson. We'll utilize the re module for this.

Before we begin, let's import it.

>>> import re

Metacharacters in Python Regex

In a Python Regex, each character is either a metacharacter or a regular character. A metacharacter has a unique meaning, whereas a standard character is a mirror image of itself.

The following metacharacters are available in Python:

Metacharacter	Description
^	Matches the start of the string
.	Matches a single character, except a newline But when used inside square brackets, a dot is matched
[ ]	A bracket expression matches a single character from the ones inside it [abc] matches 'a', 'b', and 'c' [a-z] matches characters from 'a' to 'z' [a-cx-z] matches 'a', 'b', 'c', 'x', 'y', and 'z'
[^]	Matches a single character from those except the ones mentioned in the brackets[^abc] matches all characters except 'a', 'b' and 'c'
( )	Parentheses define a marked subexpression, also called a block, or a capturing group
\t, \n, \r, \f	Tab, newline, return, form feed
*	Matches the preceding character zero or more times ab*c matches 'ac', 'abc', 'abbc', and so on [ab]* matches '', 'a', 'b', 'ab', 'ba', 'aba', and so on (ab)* matches '', 'ab', 'abab', 'ababab', and so on
{m,n}	Matches the preceding character minimum m times, and maximum n times a{2,4} matches 'aa', 'aaa', and 'aaaa'

Symbol	Description
{m}	Matches the preceding character exactly m times
?	Matches the preceding character zero or one times ab?c matches 'ac' or 'abc'
+	Matches the preceding character one or one times ab+c matches 'abc', 'abbc', 'abbbc', and so on, but not 'ac'
|	The choice operator matches either the expression before it, or the one after abc|def matches 'abc' or 'def'
\w	Matches a word character (a-zA-Z0-9) \W matches single non-word characters
\b	Matches the boundary between word and non-word characters
\s	Matches a single whitespace character \S matches a single non-whitespace character
\d	Matches a single decimal digit character (0-9)
\	A single backslash inhibits a character's specialness Examples- \. \\ * When unsure if a character has a special meaning, put a \ before it: \@
s	A dollar matches the end of the string

Backslashes are not handled in any special way by a raw string literal. To do so, add an 'r' to the beginning of the pattern.

You might have to use '' for a single backslash character if you don't have this. However, you simply need r" for this.

Characters that are similar to one another.

A Match's Rules

So, how does this function in practice? The following guidelines must be followed:

1. The search traverses the string from beginning to end.

2. The entire pattern, but not the entire string, must match.

3. The search comes to an end with the first match.

The group() technique returns the matching phrase if a match is discovered. If this is not the case, it returns None.

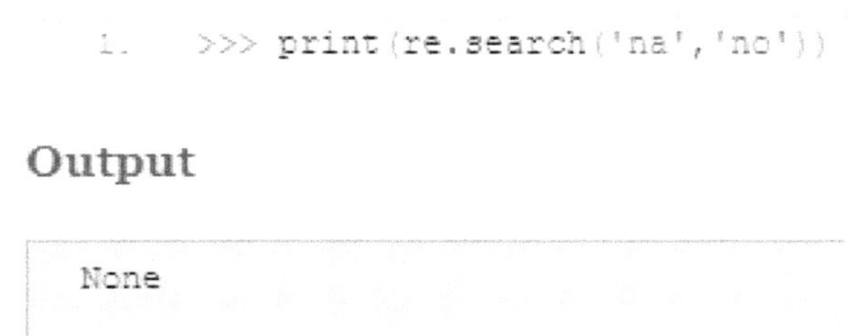

Output

```
None
```

Let's have a look at a couple of key functions right now.

Regular Expression Functions in Python

A few routines are available to aid in the use of Python regex.

1. match ()

A pattern and a string are sent to match(). It returns the string if they match. Otherwise, it will return None.

Let us look at some regular expression match examples in Python.

```
1.    >>> print(re.match('center','centre'))
```

Output

```
None
```

```
1.    >>> print(re.match('...\w\we','centre'))
```

Output

```
<_sre.SRE_Match object; span=(0, 6), match='centre'>
```

2. search()

Like match(), search() accepts two arguments: a pattern and a string to search.

Let us take a look at a couple of examples.

```
1.    >>> match=re.search('aa?yushi','ayushi')
2.    >>> match.group()
```

Output

```
'ayushi'
```

```
1.    >>> match=re.search('aa?yushi?','ayush ayushi')
2     >>> match.group()
```

Output

```
'ayush'
```

```
1.    >>> match=re.search('\w+end','Hey! What are your plans for the weekend?')
2.    >>> match.group()
```

Output

```
'weekend'
```

```
1.    >>> match=re.search('^\w+end','Hey! What are your plans for the weekend?')
2     >>> match.group()
```

OUTPUT

```
Traceback (most recent call last):File "<pyshell#337>", line 1, in <module>
match.group()
AttributeError: 'NoneType' object has no attribute 'group'
```

Because there was no match, an AttributeError was thrown. This is due to the fact that we specified that this pattern should appear at the start of the string.

Let's see if we can find some space.

```
1.    >>> match=re.search('i\sS','Ayushi Sharma')
2.    >>> match.group()
```

Output

```
'i S'
```

```
1.    >>> match=re.search('\w+c{2}\w*','Occam\'s Razor')
2.    >>> match.group()
```

Output

```
'Occam'
```

It will take some time to become accustomed to what the metacharacters signify.

But, because there aren't that many of us, it won't take long.

Regex Examples in Python

Let's attempt making an email address regex in Python. So, how does one appear to be? It appears as follows: abc-def@ghi.com

Let's take a look at the following code:

```
1.    >>> match=re.search(r'[\w.-]+@[\w-]+\.[\w]+','Please mail it to
ayushiwasthere@gmail.com')
2.    >>> match.group()
```

OUTPUT

`ayushiwasthere@gmail.com' It worked perfectly!

Here, if you would have typed [\w-.] instead of [\w.-], it would have raised the following error:

```
1.    >>> match=re.search(r'[\w-.]+@[\w-]+\.[\w]+','Please mail it to
      ayushiwasthere@gmail.com')
```

```
Traceback (most recent call last):File "<pyshell#347>", line 1, in <module>

match=re.search(r'[\w-.]+@[\w-]+\.[\w]+','Please mail it to ayushiwasthere@gmail.com')

File "C:\Users\lifei\AppData\Local\Programs\Python\Python36-32\lib\re.py", line 182, in search
return _compile(pattern, flags).search(string)

File "C:\Users\lifei\AppData\Local\Programs\Python\Python36-32\lib\re.py", line 301, in _compile
p = sre_compile.compile(pattern, flags)

File "C:\Users\lifei\AppData\Local\Programs\Python\Python36-32\lib\sre_compile.py", line 562, in
compile
p = sre_parse.parse(p, flags)

File "C:\Users\lifei\AppData\Local\Programs\Python\Python36-32\lib\sre_parse.py", line 856, in
parse
p = _parse_sub(source, pattern, flags & SRE_FLAG_VERBOSE, False)

File "C:\Users\lifei\AppData\Local\Programs\Python\Python36-32\lib\sre_parse.py", line 415, in
_parse_sub
itemsappend(_parse(source, state, verbose))

File "C:\Users\lifei\AppData\Local\Programs\Python\Python36-32\lib\sre_parse.py", line 547, in
_parse
raise source.error(msg, len(this) + 1 + len(that))

sre_constants.error: bad character range \w-. at position 1
```

This is because we usually denote a range with a dash (-).

Group Extraction

Let's stick with the email example for now. What if all you need is the username?

You can do this by passing an input (such as an index) to the group() method.

Take a look at the following:

```
1.    >>> match=re.search(r'([\w.-]+)@([\w-]+)\.([\w]+)','Please mail it to
      ayushiwasthere@gmail.com')
2.    >>> match.group()
```

Output

```
'ayushiwasthere@gmail.com'
```

```
1.    >>> match.group(1)
```

Output

```
'ayushiwasthere'
```

```
1.    >>> match.group(2)
```

Output

```
'gmail'
```

```
1.    >>> match.group(3)
```

Output

```
'com'
```

You can extract the portions you desire using parentheses. Note that we used parenthesis to divide the pattern into groups for this:

r'([\w.-]+)@([\w-]+)\.([\w]+)'

Python findall()

Python regex search() terminates at the first match, as we saw above.

However, findall() in Python provides a list of all matches found.

```
1.    >>> match=re.findall(r'advi[cs]e','I could advise you on your poem, but you would
      disparage my advice')
```

```
1.    >>> for i in match:
2.          print(i)
```

Output

```
advise
advice
```

```
1.    >>> type(match)
```

Output

```
<class 'list'>
```

findall() with Files

We've dealt with files before and understand how to read and write them. Why not make your life easier by utilizing Python's findall() function to search for all files?

To go to the desktop, we'll first use the os module. Let's see what happens.

```
1.    >>> import os
2.    >>> os.chdir('C:\\Users\\lifei\\Desktop')
3.    >>> f=open('Today.txt')
```

We have a file named Today.txt on our Desktop. These are its contents:

- DS, DBMS, ADA, OS
- CSS, HTML, jQuery, JavaScript
- C++, Python, Java
- This sem's subjects
- Now, let's call findall().

```
1.    >>> match=re.findall(r'Java[\w]*',f.read())
```

Finally, let's go over it again.

```
1.    >>> for i in match:
2.            print(i)
```

Output

```
JavaScript
Java
```

findall() with Groups

We learned how parenthesis could be used to separate a pattern into groups. Take a look at what occurs when we use Python Regex findall ().

```
1.    >>> match=re.findall(r'([\w]+)\s([\w]+)','Ayushi Sharma, Fluffy Sharma, Leo Sharma,
      Candy Sharma')
2.    >>> for i in match:
3.       print(i)
```

Output

```
('Ayushi', 'Sharma')
('Fluffy', 'Sharma')
('Leo', 'Sharma')
('Candy', 'Sharma')
```

Python Regex Options

Optional arguments may be passed to the functions we described. These are the possibilities:

1. Python Regular Expression IGNORECASE

While matching, this Python Regex ignores case ignores the case.

Consider the following Python Regex IGNORECASE:

```
1.    >>> match=re.findall(r'hi','Hi, did you ship it, Hillary?',re.IGNORECASE)
2.    >>> for i in match:
3.          print(i)
```

Output

```
Hihi

Hi
```

2. Python MULTILINE

When working with a multi-line string, this allows and $ to match the beginning and finish of each line rather than the entire string.

```
1.    >>> match=re.findall(r'^Hi','Hi, did you ship it, Hillary?\nNo, I didn\'t, but
      Hi',re.MULTILINE)
2.    >>> for i in match:
3.          print(i)
```

Output

```
Hi
```

3. Python DOTALL.

* only matches the first line; it does not scan the entire string. This is due to the fact that. Does not match a newline.

We use DOTALL to make this possible.

```
1.    >>> match=re.findall(r'.*','Hi, did you ship it, Hillary?\nNo, I didn\'t, but
      Hi',re.DOTALL)
2.    >>> for i in match:
3.          print(i)
```

Output

```
Hi, did you ship it, Hillary?No, I didn't, but Hi
```

Greedy vs Non-Greedy

The metacharacters *, +, and ? are greedy. This means that they keep searching. Let's take an example.

```
1.    >>> match=re.findall(r'(<.*>)','<em>Strong</em> <i>Italic</i>')
2.    >>> for i in match:
3.        print(i)
```

Output

```
<em></em>

<i>

</i>
```

This gave us the whole string because it greedily keeps searching. What if we just want the opening and closing tags? Look:

print(i)

```
1.    >>> match=re.findall(r'(<.*?>)','<em>Strong</em> <i>Italic</i>')
2.    >>> for i in match:
3.        print(i)
```

Output

```
<em></em>

<i>

</i>
```

The .* is greedy, and the? Makes it non-greedy.

Alternatively, we could also do this:

```
1.    >>> match=re.findall(r'</?\w+>','<em>Strong</em> <i>Italic</i>')
2.    >>> for i in match:
3.        print(i)
```

Output

```
<em></em>
<i>
</i>
```

Here's another example:

```
1.    >>> match=re.findall('(a*?)b','aaabbc')
2.    >>> for i in match:
3.        print(i)
```

Output

```
aaa
```

The? makes * non-greedy in this case. Also, if the b after the? had been skipped, the result would have been an empty string.

After the? there must be a character to stop at. *? +? and?? all work with this method.

Similarly, m,n? makes it non-greedy and matches the fewest probable instances.

Substitution The sub() function can be used to replace a part of a string with another. pattern, substring, and string are the three inputs to sub().

```
1.    >>> re.sub('^a','an','a apple')
```



```
'an apple'
```

Here, we used ^ so it won't change apple to apple. The grammar police approve.

Regex Applications in Python

So, now that we have learned a lot about Python regular expressions, where do we put them to use? They're useful in the following places:

- Internet search engines
- Replace dialogues in word processors and text editors with Find and Replace.
- Tools for text processing, such as sed and AWK
- Lexical analysis

This was the Python Regex Tutorial in its entirety.

Regular Expressions in Python Interview Questions

1. In Python, what is a regular expression? Use an example to demonstrate your point.
2. What is the difference between a regular expression and a regular expression in Python?
3. What does the question mark in a regular expression in Python mean?
4. In Python, how do you split a regular expression?
5. What is the best way to see if a regular expression is in Python?

6. These were the fundamentals of regular expressions in Python. To be honest, we think having such a tool in our arsenal is very cool.

Chapter 10. PYTHON EXCEPTION – PYTHON ERROR & IN-BUILT EXCEPTION IN PYTHON

1. Python Error – Objective

In this Python Error tutorial, we'll look at a syntax error and how to fix it. We'll also look at Python Exceptions, error messages, and the built-in exceptions in the Python programming language.

It will go over every potential Python mistake and exception to assist you in running your Python code smoothly, as there are numerous reasons to learn Python.

So, let's get started with Python Errors and Exceptions.

2. Syntax Errors in Python

When you break the rules of Python Syntax in your code, it won't run. A syntax error occurs when the following code is used.

```
>>> if 2>1 print("2")
```

Invalid syntax has caused a SyntaxError.

Because there isn't a colon following the condition, this code doesn't run. 2>1.

The message 'Syntax Error: invalid syntax' appears when a syntax error is known as a parsing error.

3. What is Python Exception?

It may be useful to identify the flaws in your Python code before putting it to use. However, this does not always occur. Sometimes errors appear when you run the code; other times, they appear in the middle of it.

A Python exception is an error that occurs during the execution of a program. It could be fatal to the program, although it isn't always the case. Let's look at the most usual scenario.

>>> a,b=1,0

>>> print(a/b)

Traceback (most recent call last):

File "<pyshell#208>", line 1, in <module>

print(a/b)

ZeroDivisionError: division by zero

So far in our python tutorials, you've come across terms like TypeError, NameError, and so on. It's past time to figure out what it is.

4. Python Error and Python Exception Message

If a Python error or exception is not handled, it prints a four-line warning on the screen.

This is a traceback, as the first line says. This signifies that the interpreter looks for the source of the Python exception.

The second number is the line number of the Python code that threw an exception. It's line 1 in our case, which implies this is the 208th sentence we've run in the interpreter since we first opened it.

The third line identifies the line (or statement) that threw the Python exception.

The fourth line finally specifies the type of Python exception that occurred. This is followed by a summary of what occurred.

5. In-built Python Exception

Now that we understand what an exception is, we'll go over a list of Python exceptions that are built-in. Try to recall if you've ever run into any of these Python exceptions as you read through the list. Let us know in the comments section.

a. AssertionError in python

When an assert statement fails, this Python exception is thrown. Python raises expression is another name for this.

The following is an example of a successful assert statement:

```
1.    >>> assert(1==1)
```

But when we write the following code, we get an AssertionError:

```
1.    >>> assert(1==2)
```

Traceback (most recent call last):

File "<pyshell#213>", line 1, in <module>

assert(1==2)

AssertionError

We'll take the assert statement in detail in a future lesson.

b. AttributeError in python

When an attribute assignment or reference fails, this error occurs. Let's take the class 'fruit' as an example.

'fruit.'

```
1.    >>> class fruit:
```

pass

```
1.    >>> fruit.size
```

(Last call) Traceback (most recent call):

Line 1 of the file "pyshell#223>" in the module "fruit. size"

AttributeError: The type object 'fruit' does not have a size attribute.

The attribute size does not exist in this case. As a result, it throws an AttributeError.

c. EOFError in Python

When the input() function encounters the end-of-file condition, this Python exception is thrown.

d. Python's FloatingPointError

This python error happens when a floating-point operation fails.

e. Python's GeneratorExit

When the close() method of a generator is called, this raises.

f. Python ImportError

An ImportError happens when the imported module
is not found.

```
1.     >>> from math import ppi
```

File "<pyshell#234>", line 1, in <module>

from math import PPI."

ImportError: The name 'ppi' could not be imported.

g. IndexErrorin Python

An IndexError occurs when you try to access an index
on a sequence that is out of range.

```
1.     >>> list=[1,2,3]
2.     >>> list[3]
```

File "<pyshell#236>", line 1, in <module>

list[3]

IndexError: list index out of range

h. KeyError in Python

When a key isn't found in a dictionary, this raises a KeyError in Python.

```
1.     >>> dict1={1:1,2:2}
2.     >>> dict1[3]
```

Traceback (most recent call last):

File "<pyshell#239>", line 1, in <module>

dict1[3]

KeyError: 3

i. KeyboardInterrupt in Python

This one occurs when the user hits the interrupt key (Ctrl + C).

```
1.      >>> while True: print("Hello")
2.      Hello
3.      Hello
4.      Hello
5.      Hello
6.      Hello
7.      Hello
8.      Hello
9.      Hello
10.     Hello
11.     Hello
12.     Hello
13.     Hello
14.     Hello
15.     Hello
16.     Hello
17.     Hello
18.     Hello
19.     Hello
20.     Hello
21.     Hello
22.     Hello
23.     Hello
```

Traceback (most recent call last):

File "<pyshell#244>", line 1, in <module>

while True: print("Hello")

KeyboardInterrupt \sj.

j. MemoryError in Python

When an action runs out of memory,

k. Python ModuleNotFoundError

The ModuleNotFoundError is thrown when you import a module that does not exist. >>> import maths

Traceback (most recent call last):

File "<pyshell#233>", line 1, in <module>

importmathematics

ModuleNotFoundError: There is no such module as 'maths.'

l. NameError in Python

A NameError occurs when a name isn't found in scope.

>>> eggs

Traceback (most recent call last):

File "<pyshell#245>", line 1, in <module>

eggs

NameError: name 'eggs' is not defined

m. Python's NotImplementedError

A NotImplementedError is thrown when an abstract technique is used.

n. OSError in Python

When a system operation results in a system-related error, this flag is now raised.

o. OverflowError in Python

When the result of an arithmetic operation is too vast to be represented, an error occurs.

p. ReferenceError in Python

When a weak reference proxy is used to access a garbage collected referent, this error is raised.

q. RuntimeError in Python

A RuntimeError is an error that does not fit into any of the other categories.

r. StopIteration in Python

The next() function sets StopIteration to signal that the iterator will not return any further items.

>>> **def** countdown():

n=4

while(n>0):

yield n

n-=1

>>> c=countdown()

>>> next(c)

4

>>> next(c)

3

>>> next(c)

2

>>> next(c)

1

>>> next(c)

Traceback (most recent call last):

File "<pyshell#23>", line 1, in <module>

next(c)

StopIteration

s. Python's IndentationError

When the indentation is incorrect, an IndentationError is thrown.

t. Python's TabError

A TabError occurs when the indentation in tabs and spaces is incorrect.

u. Python's SystemError

A system error occurs when the interpreter identifies an internal error.

v. Python's SystemExit

This is raised by the sys. exit() function.

w. Python's TypeError

A TypeError occurs when a function or operation is applied to an object of the wrong type.

>>> '10'+10'

(Last call) Traceback (most recent call):

Line 1 of the file "pyshell#38>" in the module "pyshell#38>"

'10'+10

TypeError: str, not int, must be used

x. Python's UnboundLocalError

When you attempt to access a local variable without giving it a value, you get an UnboundLocalError.

```
1.    >>> def sayhi():
2.            m+=1
3.            print(m)
4.    >>> sayhi()
```

Traceback (most recent call last):

File "<pyshell#53>", line 1, in <module>

sayhi()

File "<pyshell#52>", line 2, in sayhi

m+=1

UnboundLocalError: local variable 'm' referenced before assignment

y. UnicodeError in Python

When a Unicode-related encoding/decoding error occurs, you get the UnicodeError exception.

z. UnicodeEncodeError in Python

This is a Unicode error during encoding.

aa. UnicodeDecodeError in Python

The Unicode error during decoding is termed UnicodeDecodeError.

Ab. UnicodeTranslateError in Python

A UnicodeTranslateError occurs during translating.

Ac. ValueError in Python

You get a ValueError when you send in an argument of the correct type but an improper value.

>>> int(input())

3.5

Traceback (most recent call last):

File "<pyshell#55>", line 1, in <module>

int(input())

ValueError: invalid literal for int() with base 10: '3.5'

ad. ZeroDivisionError in Python

Finally, a ZeroDivisionError is one we've seen in section 3. When the denominator of a division is 0, this Python exception is raised. This doesn't necessarily violate syntax.

>>> print(1/0)

Traceback (most recent call last):

File "<pyshell#56>", line 1, in <module>

print(1/0)

ZeroDivisionError: division by zero

So, this is all about the Python Error and Python Exception. I hope you like our explanation.

Chapter 11. A DIVE INTO PYTHON CLOSURES AND DECORATORS

Closures are a class of Python constructs that are quite elegant. We'll learn about them, how to define a closure, and why and when to utilize closures in this post.

However, before we can understand a closure, we must first comprehend what a nested function is and how scoping constraints apply to it. So, let's get this party started.

Python Scoping Rules and Nested Functions

When a function is run, a new local namespace reflects the local environment and contains the names of function parameters and variables assigned within the function body. A namespace can be compared to a dictionary, with the keys being the object names and the values being the objects themselves.

The interpreter searches the local namespace first when resolving names. If no match is found, the global namespace, the module where the function is defined, is searched. If no match is discovered, the built-in namespace is checked before the NameError exception is raised. This is depicted in the diagram below:

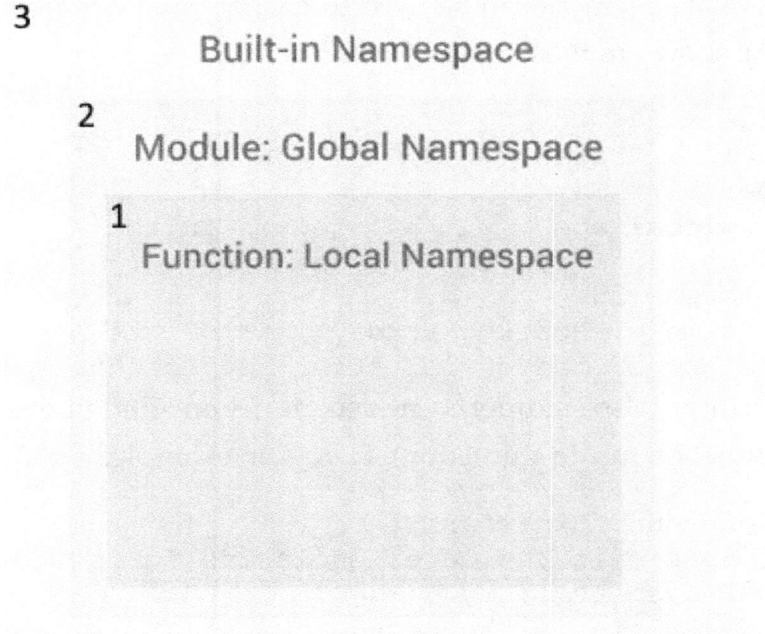

Namespace search order by Python Interpreter

Let's consider the below example:

```
age = 27
def birthday():
  age = 28birthday()
print(age)  # age will still be 27
>>
27
```

Variables given inside a function have always been bound to the function's local namespace; as a result, the variable age in the technique body refers to a new object with the value 28, not the outside variable. The global statement can be used to change this behavior. As shown in the example below:

```
age = 27
name = "Sarah"
def birthday():
  global age        # 'age' is in the
global namespace
  age = 28
  name = "Roark"birthday()            # age
is now 28. name will still be "Sarah".
```

Python also supports nested function definitions (function inside a function). Here's an example:

```
def countdown(start):
  # This is the outer enclosing function
def display():
    # This is the nested function
    n = start
    while n > 0:
      n-=1
      print('T-minus %d' % n)
```

```
    display()# We execute the function
countdown(3)
>>>
T-minus 3
T-minus 2
T-minus 1
```

Defining a Closure Function

What if the last lines of the function countdown()
provided the display function instead of calling it in the
previous example? This indicates that the function was
written as follows:

```
def countdown(start):
  # This is the outer enclosing function
def display():
    # This is the nested function
    n = start
    while n > 0:
      n-=1
      print('T-minus %d' % n)    return
display# Now let's try calling this
function.
counter1 = countdown(2)
counter1()
>>>
```

```
T-minus 2
T-minus 1
```

With the value two as a parameter, the countdown() function was called, and the resultant function was given the name counter1. When counter1() is called, the value of start passed to countdown is used (). As a result, even though we had previously completed the countdown() function, the value was still remembered when calling counter1().

The closure is the Python term for attaching some data (2 in this case) to the code.

Even if the variable goes out of scope or the function is removed from the current namespace, the value in the surrounding scope is remembered. To be sure, let's run the following code:

```
>>> del countdown>>> counter1()
T-minus 2
T-minus 1>>> countdown(2)
Traceback (most recent call last):
...
NameError: name 'countdown' is not
defined
```

When should you use closures?

Closures can give an alternative and more elegant way when only a few techniques are implemented in a class (usually just one). Closures and nested functions are also particularly beneficial when writing code that uses the lazy or delayed evaluation idea. Here's an illustration:

```python
from urllib.request import urlopendef page(url):
  def get():
    return urlopen(url).read()
  return get
```

The page() function in the preceding example does not do any calculations. Instead, it simply generates and returns the function get(), which, when called, fetches the contents of a web page. As a result, the computation performed by getting () is postponed in the program when getting () is evaluated. Consider the following scenario:

```python
>>> url1 = page("http://www.google.com")
>>> url2 = page("http://www.bing.com")
>>> url1
<function page.<locals>.get at
0x10a6054d0>
>>> url2
<function page.<locals>.get at
0x10a6055f0>

>>> gdata = url1()      # Fetches
http://www.google.com
>>> bdata = url2()      # Fetches
http://www.bing.com
>>>
```

It is possible to determine the values that are enclosed in the closure function.

If a function is a closure function, it has a __closure__ attribute which returns a tuple of cell objects. We know that url1 and url2 are closure functions from the previous example.

```
>>> page.__closure__              # Returns None since not a closure
>>> url1.__closure__
(<cell at 0x10a5f1250: str object at 0x10a5f3120>,)
```

The closed value is stored in the cell contents attribute of the cell object.

```
>>> url1.__closure__[0].cell_contents
'http://www.google.com'>>>
url2.__closure__[0].cell_contents
'http://www.bing.com'
```

In Python, a nested function is closed when it refers to a value in its enclosing scope. Closures help to obscure data to some extent. A closure can also be a useful tool for maintaining state consistency over several function calls. Follow these steps to create a closure function in Python:

- We'll need a nested function.

- The enclosing function must return the nested function, and the nested function must refer to a value defined in the enclosing function.

Chapter 12. NUMPY ARRAY

Python SciPy was the subject of our previous Python Library tutorial. Now we'll look at NumPy, a Python package.

We'll go over the features, installation, and NumPy ndarray in this NumPy tutorial.

In addition, we'll go through NumPy's data types and arrays. Let's get started with the Python NumPy Tutorial.

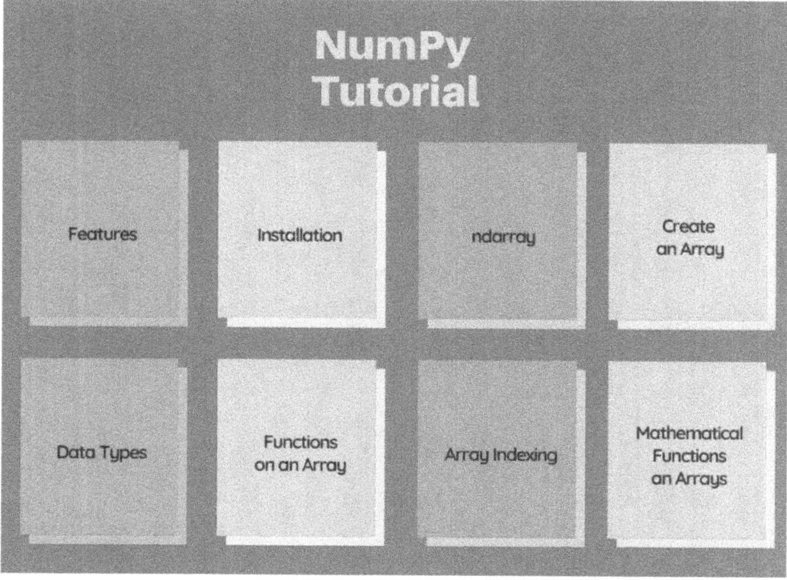

What exactly is NumPy?

NumPy is a Python package that allows you to work with large, multidimensional matrices and arrays.

It also includes several high-level functions for performing mathematical operations on these structures.

Python NumPy is a cross-platform Python interpreter with a BSD license. It's frequently used in conjunction with Matplotlib and SciPy.

This can be viewed as a replacement for MATLAB. The phrase 'Numpy' is a combination of the words 'NUMerical' and 'PYthon.'

Numpy Tutorial - Numpy Features

In this Python NumPy Tutorial, we'll look at the following NumPy features:

- NumPy is based on CPython, a bytecode interpreter that is not optimized.

- Arrays with several dimensions.
- These arrays' functions and operations
- Python is a MATLAB alternative.
- ndarray is an acronym for n-dimensional arrays.
- Manipulation of shapes and Fourier transforms
- Linear algebra and the production of random numbers

How to Install NumPy in a Numpy Tutorial

Numpy can be installed with pip.

- install numpy using pip

You may then import it as- >>> as np import NumPy

NumPy ndarray Numpy Tutorial

This is one of numpy's most important features. ndarray is an n-dimensional array, which is a grid of similar values.

This tuple is indexed by a tuple of nonnegative integers. The number of dimensions in an array determines its rank.

Let's look at a couple of examples.

```
>>> a=np.array([1,2,3])
```

```
>>> type(a)
```

Output

```
<class 'numpy.ndarray'>
```

```
>>> a.shape
```

Output

```
(3,)
```

```
>>> a[0],a[2]
```

Output

```
(1, 3)
```

```
>>> a[1]=5
```

```
>>> a
```

Output

```
array([1, 5, 3])
```

The array's shape, as you can see, is rectangular (3,). What happens when we create a multi-dimensional array?

Let's see.

```
>>> b=np.array([[2,7,9],[5,1,3]])
```

```
>>> b
```

Output

```
array([[2, 7, 9],
[5, 1, 3]])
```

>>> b[0,1]

Output

```
7
```

>>> b.shape

Output

```
(2, 3)
```

>>> b.size

Output

```
6
```

1. How to Create NumPy Array?

The lines of code that follow build a couple more arrays:

```
1.    >>> np.arange(7) #This is like range in Python
```

Output

```
array([0, 1, 2, 3, 4, 5, 6])
```

```
1.    >>> np.random.random((3,3)) #Fills in random values
```

Output

```
array([[0.56074267, 0.67303599, 0.65973007],
[0.37222497, 0.13230271, 0.40858618],
[0.74455771, 0.52119999, 0.6927821 ]])
```

1. `>>> np.ones((2,3))`

Output

```
array([[1., 1., 1.],
[1., 1., 1.]])
```

1. `>>> np.zeros((1,2))`

Output

```
array([[0., 0.]])
```

1. `>>> np.eye(3) #Identity matrix`

Output

```
array([[1., 0., 0.],
[0., 1., 0.],
[0., 0., 1.]])
```

1. `>>> np.full((3,2),7) #Matrix of constants`

Output

```
array([[7, 7],
[7, 7],
[7, 7]])
```

1. `>>> np.linspace(1,2,4) #4 values spaced evenly between, and including, 1 and 2.`

Output

```
array([1. , 1.33333333, 1.66666667, 2. ])
```

```
1.    >>> np.empty([2,3]) #Empty array
```

Output

```
array([[1., 0., 3.],
[0., 4., 0.]])
```

1. Some Parameters

```
1.    >>> np.array([1,3,4],ndmin=3) #Minimum dimension
```

Output

```
array([[[1, 3, 4]]])
```

```
1.    >>> np.array([1,3,4],dtype=complex) #Data type
```

Output

```
array([1.+0.j, 3.+0.j, 4.+0.j])
```

Numpy Tutorial – Data Types

As previously stated, a NumPy array contains members of the same type.

If you don't provide the data type while building a NumPy array, NumPy will decide for you.

The following data types are available:

bool_, int_, intc, intp, int8, int16, int32, int64, uint8, uint16, uint32, uint64, float_, float16, float32, float64, complex_, complex64, complex128

We can confirm:

```
1.    >>> np.dtype(np.int32)
```

Output

```
dtype('int32')
```

```
1.    >>> np.dtype('i4')
```

Output

```
dtype('int32')
```

```
1.    >>> np.dtype('i8')
```

Output

```
dtype('int64')
```

Functions of NumPy Array

Let's look at what we can accomplish with an array and what else we can learn from it.

```
>>> a=np.array([[1,2,3],[4,5,6]])
```

        >>> a.reshape(3,2)

Output

        array([[1, 2],
        [3, 4],
        [5, 6]])
        >>> a.ndim #Number of array dimensions

Output

```
2
```

```
1.    >>> np.array([[1,2,3],[4,5,6]]).itemsize #Length of each element in bytes
```

Output

```
4
```

```
1.    >>> np.array([[1,2,3],[4,5,6]],dtype=np.int8).itemsize
```

Output

1

>>> a

Output

```
array([[1, 2, 3],
 [4, 5, 6]])
```

```
1.    >>> a.flags
```

Output

```
C_CONTIGUOUS: True
F_CONTIGUOUS: False
OWNDATA: True
WRITEABLE: True
ALIGNED: True
WRITEBACKIFCOPY: False
UPDATEIFCOPY: False
```

Numpy Array Indexing

NumPy arrays can be sliced, with numerous slices
available for multidimensional arrays.

```
1.    >>> a=np.array([[1,2,3],[4,5,6],[7,8,9]])
2.    >>> b=a[:2,1:3]
3.    >>> b
```

Output

```
array([[2, 3],
 [5, 6]])
```

```
1.    >>> a[1,2]
```

Output

6

```
>>> b[0,0]=79
```

```
>>> a
```

Output

```
array([[ 1, 79,  3],
       [ 4,  5,  6],
       [ 7,  8,  9]])
```

Changes to a slice, as you can see, alter the original.

```
>>> a[1,:]
Output
array([4, 5, 6])
>>> a[1:2,:]
Output
array([[4, 5, 6]])
>>> a[:,1]
Output
array([79, 5, 8])
```

1. Integer Indexing

It's possible to make an array out of another array.

```
1.   >>> a=np.array([[1,2],[3,4],[5,6]])
2.   >>> a[[0,1,2],[0,1,0]] #Prints elements at [0,0], [1,1], and [2,0]
```

Output

array([1, 4, 5])

Let's pick elements-

```
1.    >>> a = np.array([[1,2,3], [4,5,6], [7,8,9], [10, 11, 12]])
2.    >>> b = np.array([0, 2, 0, 1])
3.    >>> b
```

Output

array([0, 2, 0, 1])

>>> a[np.arange(4), b]

Output

array([1, 6, 7, 11])

>>> a[np.arange(4), b]+=10

>>> a

Output

```
array([[11,  2,  3],
 [ 4,  5, 16],
 [17,  8,  9],
 [10, 21, 12]])
```

2. Boolean Indexing

This will allow you to select elements that meet a set of criteria.

>>> a=np.array([[1,2],[3,4],[5,6]])
>>> boolean=(a>3)
>>> boolean

Output

```
array([[False, False],
 [False, True],
 [ True, True]])
```

>>> a[boolean]

Output

```
array([4, 5, 6])
```

Mathematical Functions on Arrays in NumPy

Now let's look at some mathematical functions that can be used with arrays.

```
1.    >>> a=np.array([[1,2,3],[4,5,6]])
2.    >>> b=np.array([[7,8,9],[10,11,12]])
3.    >>> np.add(a,b) #a+b does the same
```

Output

```
array([[ 8, 10, 12],
 [14, 16, 18]])
```

```
1.    >>> np.subtract(a,b) #Same as a-b
```

Output

```
array([[-6, -6, -6],
 [-6, -6, -6]])
```

```
1.    >>> np.multiply(a,b) #a*b works too
```

Output

```
array([[ 7, 16, 27],
 [40, 55, 72]])
```

1.   >>> np.divide(a,b) #Same as a/b

Output

```
array([[0.14285714, 0.25 , 0.33333333],
 [0.4 , 0.45454545, 0.5 ]])
```

1.   >>> np.sqrt(a) #Produces square root

Output

Output

```
10
```

1.   >>> np.sum(a,axis=0) #Sum of each column

Output

```
array([4, 6])
```

1.   >>> np.sum(a,axis=1) #Sum of each row

Output

```
array([3, 7])
```

To transpose this matrix:

>>> a.T

Output

```
array([[1, 3],
 [2, 4]])
```

```
1.    >>> np.array([1,3,2]).T #NOP
```

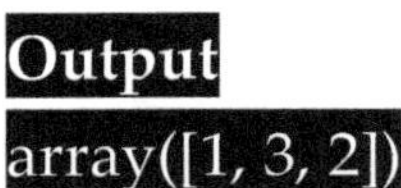

Some functions that work on a broader scale-

```
1.    >>> x=np.array([[1,2],[3,4]])
2.    >>> y=np.array([[5,6],[7,8]])
3.    >>> v=np.array([9,10])
4.    >>> w=np.array([11,12])
5.    >>> v.dot(w) #Same as np.dot(v,w)
```

Output

219

>>> x.dot(v)

Output

array([29, 67])

>>> x.dot(y)

Output

array([[19, 22],
[43, 50]])

So that was all there was to it for the Python NumPy Tutorial. I hope you found our explanation to be helpful.

NumPy Python Interview

1. What is a NumPy array in Python?

2. What is NumPy's function in Python?

3. What is the difference between Python's Pandas and NumPy?

4. What is the Python implementation of NumPy?

5. What Python functions does NumPy provide?

Conclusion

As a result, in this Python NumPy Tutorial, we looked at how to install NumPy and use NumPy ndarray.

We also talked about NumPy Array and its functions and data types. That's all there is to NumPy.

Chapter 13. PANDAS IN PYTHON

The Python-based data analysis toolbox pandas (all lowercase) can be imported using import pandas as PD. It includes various tools, from parsing numerous file formats to transforming an entire data table into a NumPy matrix array. As a result, a panda is a reliable partner in data science and machine learning.

Pandas, like NumPy, primarily work with data in 1-D and 2-D arrays, but the two are handled differently.

Series

1-D arrays are referred to as a series in pandas. The PD.Series constructor, which includes a lot of optional arguments, is used to generate a series. The data argument is the most common, as it provides the constituents of the series.

A pandas series, like NumPy arrays, uses the dtype keyword to perform manual casting.

```python
import pandas as pd

import numpy as np

ser = pd.Series()

print('{}\n'.format(ser))

ser = pd.Series(10)

print('{}\n'.format(ser))

ser = pd.Series([0, 10, 20, 30, 40, 50, 60, 70, 8
0, 90])

print('{}\n'.format(ser))

ser = pd.Series([20, 15.7, '10'])

print('{}\n'.format(ser))

# A series from a numpy array

arr = np.array([0, 10, 20, 30, 40, 50])

ser = pd.Series(arr, dtype = np.double)

print('{}\n'.format(ser))

ser = pd.Series([[15, 4], [89, 23.5], [21, 22]])

print('{}\n'.format(ser))
```

There are integers on the left side of the Series elements in the code above. The index of the series is a collection of these integers.

Indexing

As long as the index is the same length as the Series, it

can be created.

```
import pandas as pd

ser = pd.Series([1, 2, 3], index = ['first', 'second', 'third'])

print('{}\n'.format(ser))
```

```python
ser = pd.Series([50.45, 71, 90], index = [-
7, 'second', 18.7])

print('{}\n'.format(ser))
```

Run

DataFrame

A DataFrame is nothing more than a two-dimensional array. It's made with the PD.DataFrame constructor, which takes the same arguments as the PD.Series constructor. A DataFrame, on the other hand, cannot be built from a scalar (representing a single value Series).

A DataFrame's index (row) and column labels can be specified in the constructor.

```
 4
 5
 6
 7
 8
 9
10
11
12
13
14
15
16
17
18
19
import pandas as pd

df = pd.DataFrame()

print('{}\n'.format(df))

df = pd.DataFrame([20, 100, -30])

print('{}\n'.format(df))
```

```python
df = pd.DataFrame([18, -12], [54, 72])

print('{}\n'.format(df))

df = pd.DataFrame([[18, -12], [54, 72]],
                  index=['row1', 'row2'],
                  columns=['column1', 'column2'])

print('{}\n'.format(df))

df = pd.DataFrame({'a': [18, -
12], 'b': [54, 72]},
                  index=['x', 'y'])

print('{}\n'.format(df))
```

Run

Changes and deletions

The append technique, which accepts either a series or another DataFrame, can be used to add rows to a DataFrame. When dealing with a series, we must either specify the index or use the ignore index keyword. If ignore index=True is set, the row labels will be replaced with integer indexes.

The append technique does not change the original DataFrame. Instead, a new DataFrame is produced with the appended row.

The process of dropping

In a DataFrame, we may use the drop technique to delete columns and rows. One of 2 techniques can be used to accomplish this:

1. Specify the labels of the rows/columns to be dropped using the labels option. To drop from the rows or columns axis, use the labels keyword argument with the axis keyword argument (with a default value of 0).

2. Without needing to utilize the axis, give the labels of the rows or columns directly using the index or columns keyword parameters.

- Append
- Drop

```python
import pandas as pd

df = pd.DataFrame([[10, 20, 30], [40, 50, 60]])

ser = pd.Series([70, 80, 90], name='new row')

print('{}\n'.format(df))

df2 = df.append(ser)

print('{}\n'.format(df2))

df3 = df.append(ser, ignore_index = True)

print('{}\n'.format(df3))
```

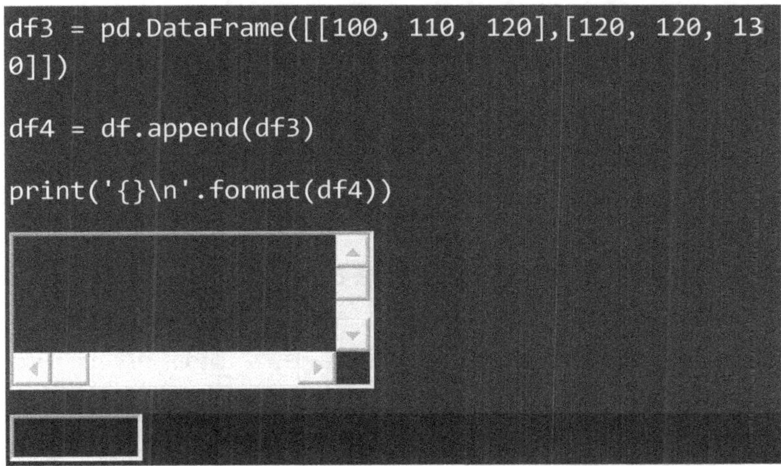

Run

Drop, like append, creates a new DataFrame.

The Concat function can be used to join DataFrames together. Merge merges two DataFrames by using all of their shared column labels.

Additional services

Pandas include a large collection of data analysis tools that let us aggregate, sort, filter, and characterize a dataset. The pyplot API can also be used to visualize DataFrames.

Chapter 14. PYTHON GENERATORS

Python's generators

Building an iterator in Python takes a lot of effort. We must create a class containing the techniques __iter__() and __next__(), maintain track of internal states and raise StopIteration when no values are to be returned.

This is both lengthy and perplexing. In such cases, the generator comes to the rescue.

Iterators can be easily created with Python generators. All of the work indicated above is completed automatically via Python generators.

A generator, in simple terms, is a function that returns an object (iterator) that we may iterate through (one value at a time).

Create Generators in Python

Creating a generator in Python is a breeze. This is the same as creating a regular function; only you'll use a yield statement instead of a return statement.

Suppose there is at least one yield statement in it (it may also have other yield or return statements). Both yield and return will return a value from a function. The distinction is that a return statement closes a function completely, whereas a yield statement pauses it and saves all of its states before continuing on subsequent calls.

What are the differences between the Generator and Normal functions?

A generator function differs from a regular function in the following ways.

- One or more yield statements can be found in the Generator function.
- When called, it returns an object (iterator), but it does not immediately begin operation.
- Techniques like __iter__() and __next__() are automatically implemented. As a result, we can use next to iterate through the objects ().

- When the function yields, it is paused, and control is handed over to the caller.
- Between calls, local variables and their states are remembered.
- Finally, when the function finishes, StopIteration is automatically raised on further calls.

Here's an example that exemplifies all of the preceding concepts. My gen() is a generator function containing numerous yield statements.

```python
# A simple generator function
def my_gen():
    n = 1
    print('This is printed first')
    # Generator function contains yield statements
    yield n

    n += 1
    print('This is printed second')
    yield n

    n += 1
    print('This is printed at last')
    yield n
```

An interactive run in the interpreter is given below. Run these in the Python shell to see the output.

```
>>> # It returns an object but does not start execution immediately.
>>> a = my_gen()

>>> # We can iterate through the items using next().
>>> next(a)
This is printed first
1
>>> # Once the function yields, the function is paused and the control is transferred

>>> # Local variables and theirs states are remembered between successive calls.
>>> next(a)
This is printed second
2

>>> next(a)
This is printed at last
3

>>> # Finally, when the function terminates, StopIteration is raised automatically o
>>> next(a)
Traceback (most recent call last):
...
StopIteration
>>> next(a)
Traceback (most recent call last):
...
StopIteration
```

It's worth noting that the value of variable n is maintained between calls in the preceding example.

The local variables aren't destroyed when the function yields, unlike conventional functions. In addition, the generator object can only be iterated once.

To restart the process, use something like a = my gen to generate a new generator object ().

Last but not least, generators can be used directly with for loops.

This is because a for loop takes an iterator and uses the next() function to traverse it. When StopIteration is raised, it automatically ends. To learn how a for loop is implemented in Python, see here.

```python
# A simple generator function
def my_gen():
    n = 1
    print('This is printed first')
    # Generator function contains yield statements
    yield n

    n += 1
    print('This is printed second')
    yield n

    n += 1
    print('This is printed at last')
    yield n


# Using for loop
for item in my_gen():
    print(item)
```

When you run the program, the output will be:

```
This is printed first
1
This is printed second
2
This is printed at last
3
```

Generators in Python with a Loop

The preceding example is less useful, and we looked at it only to understand what was going on in the background.

Generator functions are often built using a loop with an appropriate ending condition.

Let's look at a generator that reverses a string as an example.

```python
def rev_str(my_str):
    length = len(my_str)
    for i in range(length - 1, -1, -1):
        yield my_str[i]


# For loop to reverse the string
for char in rev_str("hello"):
    print(char)
```

Output

```
o
l
l
e
h
```

The range() function was used in this example to acquire the index in reverse order using the for a loop.

Not only does this generator function work with strings, but it also works with other types of iterables like list, tuple, and so on.

Python Expression Generator

Generator expressions make it simple to design simple generators on the fly. It simplifies the process of creating generators.

Generator expressions work similarly to lambda functions in that they construct anonymous generator functions.

The syntax of a generator expression in Python is identical to that of a list comprehension. However, instead of square brackets, round parenthesis is used.

The main distinction between a list comprehension and a generator expression is that the former creates the complete list while the latter produces one item at a time.

They are sloppy in their execution (producing items only when asked for). As a result, a generator expression uses far less memory than a list comprehension.

```python
# Initialize the list
my_list = [1, 3, 6, 10]

# square each term using list comprehension
list_ = [x**2 for x in my_list]

# same thing can be done using a generator expression
# generator expressions are surrounded by parenthesis ()
generator = (x**2 for x in my_list)

print(list_)
print(generator)
```

Output

```
[1, 9, 36, 100]
<generator object <genexpr> at 0x7f5d4eb4bf50>
```

As we can see from the example above, the generator expression did not give the desired output right away. It instead returned a generator object, which only makes objects when they are requested.

The following is how we can begin receiving stuff from the generator:

```python
# Initialize the list
my_list = [1, 3, 6, 10]

a = (x**2 for x in my_list)
print(next(a))

print(next(a))

print(next(a))

print(next(a))

next(a)
```

We receive the following output when we run the aforementioned program:

```
1
9
36
100
Traceback (most recent call last):
  File "<string>", line 15, in <module>
StopIteration
```

As function arguments, generator expressions can be used. The round parenthesis can be dropped when used in this way.

```
>>> sum(x**2 for x in my_list)
146

>>> max(x**2 for x in my_list)
100
```

Utilization of Python Generators

Generators are a strong implementation for a variety of reasons.

1. It's Simple to Implement

In comparison to their iterator class cousin, generators can be constructed straightforwardly and concisely. The following is an example of using an iterator class to implement a power of two sequences.

```python
class PowTwo:
    def __init__(self, max=0):
        self.n = 0
        self.max = max

    def __iter__(self):
        return self

    def __next__(self):
        if self.n > self.max:
            raise StopIteration

        result = 2 ** self.n
        self.n += 1
        return result
```

The preceding presentation was lengthy and perplexing. Let's try it again with a generator function.

```python
def PowTwoGen(max=0):
    n = 0
    while n < max:
        yield 2 ** n
        n += 1
```

The implementation was concise and considerably cleaner because generators kept care of information automatically.

2. Memory Powerful

Before returning the result, a regular function that returns a sequence will build the full sequence in memory. If the number of elements in the sequence is huge, this is overkill.

Using a generator to implement such sequences saves memory and is preferred because it only produces one item at a time.

3. Infinite Stream Representation

Generators are great for representing an endless stream of data. Infinite streams cannot be stored in memory, but generators can represent an infinite stream of data because they only produce one item at a time.

The generator function below can generate all even numbers (at least in theory).

```python
def all_even():
    n = 0
    while True:
        yield n
        n += 2
```

4. Pipelining Generators

A set of processes can be pipelined using multiple generators. An example is the greatest way to demonstrate this.

Assume we have a machine that generates numbers from the Fibonacci sequence. We also have a generator that squares numbers.

If we wish to compute the sum of squares of integers in the Fibonacci series, we can pipe the output of generator functions together in the following technique.

```python
def fibonacci_numbers(nums):
    x, y = 0, 1
    for _ in range(nums):
        x, y = y, x+y
        yield x

def square(nums):
    for num in nums:
        yield num**2

print(sum(square(fibonacci_numbers(10))))
```

Output

```
4895
```

This pipelining is effective and simple to read (not to mention a lot cooler!).

Chapter 15.
BRANCHING

Conditional branching is a fundamental aspect of programming. When a program branches, it decides whether or not to do something.

Making a branch If you're using Python, study the logic.

A program doesn't just determine whether or not to perform something on the spur of the moment: we rely on the reliable realm of logic.

The powerful 'if' sentence is where it all starts. A condition is similar to a loop in appearance, but it only executes once. If a condition is True, the if statement checks it. If it is, it executes the following indented code (remember, we use four spaces instead of a tab to indent our code):

if it's true, print ("Hello World")

When you run this program, it will display the message "Hello World." Change the if condition to False:

if the answer is False:

to be printed ("Hello World")

...and as a result, nothing will happen.

You can't just type True or False, of course. Instead, you define a condition that evaluates True or False; the equals sign (==) is a common example. This determines if two things on either side are identical. Make a new file and paste the password1.py code into it.

Password.py

```python
password = "qwerty"

attempt = input("Enter password: ")

if attempt == password:

    print("Welcome")
```

This code is a basic program that asks you to enter a password; if you input the proper password, 'qwerty,' it displays 'Welcome.' Make sure you don't get the equals logic operator == mixed up with the single equals symbol =. The double equals sign ensures that both sides are equal, whereas the single equals sign ensures that both sides are equal. For new developers, getting == and = mixed up is a common blunder.

In Python, branching is done by utilizing the If Else statement.

The next conditional branch control to learn after it is 'else.' This command is a companion to if, and it acts as a substitute. It executes when if the branch is True, and the other branch executes when it is False.

```python
if True:
    print("The first branch ran")
else:
    print("The second branch ran")
```

Run this program and you'll see 'The first branch ran'. But change True to False:

```python
if False:
    print("The first branch ran")
else:
    print("The second branch ran")
```

...and you'll see 'The second branch ran'. Let's use this to expand our password program. Enter the code from password2.py. **Password2.py**

```python
password = "qwerty"
attempt = input("Enter password: ")

if attempt == password:
    print("Welcome")
else:
    print("Incorrect password!")
```

Restart the program. You'll get a welcome message if you get the password right now. If you don't, you'll get an error notice that says "incorrect password."

Use If, Else, and Elif for more intelligent code.

'elif' is the third branching statement you should be aware of. This sentence fits between the if and else statements and stands for "else if." Consider the following elif statement. Please enter the following code:

```python
if False:
    print("The first block of code ran")
elif True:
    print("The second block of code ran")
else:
    print("The third block of code ran")
```

When you run this program, you will notice that it skips the first if expression but executes the elif statement instead. You will get a message that says, "The second block of code ran." The otherwise statement has no True or False condition; it executes as long as neither the if nor the elif statements are True. (Note that the else sentence is optional; you can just use if and elif instead.) What happens if both the if and elif conditions are set to True? Give it a shot and see whether only if, elif, or both runs. Play around with eliminating the else statement and see what happens. It will assist you in understanding the if, elif, and other expressions.

Workplace branching: Python code to make FizzBuzz

We'll show you a software that's commonly used in computer programming interviews. It's called 'FizzBuzz,' demonstrating that you know what if, else, and elif statements are. To begin, you must understand the modulo operator (percent). This is comparable to the divide operator and is used to get the remaining from a division. Consider the following function:

```
10 / 4 == 2.5
```
If we use a modulo instead, we get this:
```
10 % 4 == 2
```
Modulo turns out to be handy in lots of ways. You can use % 2 to figure out if a number is odd or even:
```
10 % 2 == 0 # this is even
11 % 2 == 1 # this is odd
```

This program works out if a number is even or odd:

```python
number = 10

if number % 2 == 0:
    print("The number is even")
else:
    print("The number is odd")
```

Code your FizzBuzz program in Python

Our FizzBuzz was tasked with printing numbers ranging from 1 to 100. Print 'Fizz' instead of the number if the number is divisible by three (such as 6, 3, or 9); if the number is divisible by five, print 'Buzz' instead of the number.

However, if a number is divisible by both 3 and 5, such as 15, you should print 'FizzBuzz.'

In FizzBuzz, we're introducing you to a new element: the 'and' statement. This determines whether two conditions are met: the number can be divided by both 3 and 5. If both conditions are true, it returns True.

And, or, and not are the three major logical operators. The first two are fairly self-explanatory, but the 'not' operator can be a bit perplexing at first. Don't stress about it; with practice, you'll get the feel of it.

Use the fizzbuzz.py code to practice utilizing logical operators and the if, else, and elif parts.

fizzbuzz.py

```python
count = 1
end = 100

while count <= end:
    if count % 5 == 0 and count % 3 == 0:
        print("FizzBuzz")
    elif count % 3 == 0:
        print("Fizz")
    elif count % 5 == 0:
        print("Buzz")
    else:
        print(count)

    count += 1
```

Python's logical operators

Logical operators can be used to combine conditions. You have three logical operators at your disposal:

and True for both operands:

or (a and b) is True for any operator: (a) or (b) is correct.

not Checks whether something is true or not: If both a and b are False, not (a and b) is True.

Learn how to comment on your Python code.

Using comments in your programs is a sign of a good programmer. Humans can understand parts of your program, thanks to comments. The computer completely disregards them. A hash symbol (#) is used to start a comment line in Python. It might be on its line or immediately following a line of code. Python will stop translating anything that comes after the # into machine code as soon as it reaches the #.

```python
# This is a comment. The whole line is ignored by the program
# The print statement will run, as it has no comment

print("Hello World")

print("Goodbye World") # This is also a comment. But print() runs
```

CONCLUSION

Now that you've learned all the most relevant Python commands, you're ready to dive into this extraordinary world dominated by creativity.

Python is a more "high-level" programming language than most other object-oriented languages, suitable for, among other uses, developing distributed applications, scripting, numerical computation and system testing.

Thanks to this manual, you'll be able to juggle the various commands and create your first programs.

Therefore, it only remains for me to wish you a lot of fun!

If you want to take a look at the most basic commands and give a dusting to the first rudiments to make your knowledge more solid and secure, or if you want to know some tutorials and various practical applications, I recommend you read the other manuals in the series:

- **GET STARTED PROGRAMMING WITH PYTHON**
- **BASIC PYTHON COMMANDS**
- **PYTHON PRACTICAL APPLICATIONS and**
- **PYTHON TUTORIALS.**

www.ingramcontent.com/pod-product-compliance
Lightning Source LLC
Chambersburg PA
CBHW060818050726
47601CB00013B/110

9 781914 599866